MW01174413

THE MAPLE TREE

TRACY L GILBERT

The Maple Tree
Copyright © 2021 by Tracy L Gilbert

Tellwell Talent
www.tellwell.ca

ISBN
978-0-2288-4647-5 (Hardcover)
978-0-2288-4648-2 (Paperback)
978-0-2288-4646-8 (eBook)

This book is dedicated to my son Jordan Burns and his fiancée Shayna for encouraging me to publish this book.

To my friends and Family, such as Ronald Solley for always being there for me. Last, but not least Rob Wall for believing in me. Thank you.

Once upon a time, I was in a dark place. I could hear a voice, and he seemed to be talking to me. I heard him say, "This seed is going to be planted in the very best soil to grow the perfect tree."

I do not know how long it was, but it seemed like forever in the dark. I just hoped there would be light soon. The man's voice kept saying, "Any day now I will meet my new friend."

Then one day or night, I felt myself growing. My head popped out of the soil, and there was light. I started looking at everything. There were other trees and plenty of flowers; I was no longer alone.

Suddenly, I heard a voice: "Hello, are you new here too? Oh, geez, that is a silly question," he laughed. "I watched your head pop up. I myself got to see the light yesterday. I should have waited and you and I would have had the same birthday."

"Where am I?" I asked.

"Well, you are here," said Oakley.

"Where is here?" It looked like a warm friendly place, and it had sounded friendly while I was in the dark.

"Oh, ha! Well, you are in a nursery. They call it a greenhouse. Oh, and there is a man who talks to us. People call him Mr. Green Leaf. Didn't you hear the voice in the dark?"

I looked around. Mr. Green Leaf had planted me in a beautiful pot in the perfect soil in a lovely nursery. I guessed that I would grow to be the perfect tree. Mr. Green Leaf would water us every day. He was so proud of all his seeds. He started calling us his beautiful seedlings.

He talked to us every day. He really loved me. He would always smile at me and say, "You are going to be a beautiful and proud maple tree."

As I grew bigger and stronger, I would communicate with the all the other plants in the nursery. Oakley the oak tree was so funny that I think his name should be Jokely as he was always telling jokes. Elm was a slippery little tree, and Weeping Willow cried a lot. Oh, Pine and Spruce mostly stayed to themselves, and at night they would talk about being very special trees that would be decorated and given lots of presents during a holiday called Christmas. I guess that is what Mr. Green Leaf told them, just like he told me I was a very special tree. He said that people would treat me with respect. He also told me my leaf is on a flag representing a great country called Canada.

This was much better than being in the dark. Mr. Green Leaf always told stories. He always said to himself, "If I talk to my beautiful trees and plants, they will feel the love and they will grow big and strong." He would then say, "Goodnight, my beauties."

When the lights were turned off, these dim lights came on and boy were these trees and plants noisy. They all started talking at once.

"Hello, hello there, excuse me," I said, and then they all stopped. "Hi, I am new here and want to be your friend, but I can't hear anything if you all talk at once. We are just talking over each other. Could we all take turns talking?"

"That's a good idea. I will go first," Oakley said.

"No you won't," Elm shouted out. "I am the eldest tree in here and the tree before me told me that this story must be passed on before I go." He looked at Buddy the Birch. "After me, it will be your turn, Buddy, and so on, and so on. Yes, some of you have heard this story before, but it must be told to the newbies — not only to save them from the sadness, but to let them know all the good that comes from being here."

Elm continued, "Pay attention, as one day you will have to tell this story. Have any of you noticed the people who come into the nursery and give Mr. Green Leaf paper? And in exchange, Mr. Green Leaf gives them one of us? Well, that paper is also known as money. People exchange this paper for us."

"Where do I get mine? The money, I mean," Oakley interrupted and laughed.

Elm gave Oakley an evil eye and continued, "The most important thing in this story is that Mr. Green Leaf has given us a wonderful home where we have met wonderful friends. Don't be sad when they go, as they will discover a beautiful world out there. Be happy for them; they are still happy. Now plants, the rest of the story is more for the trees, so go ahead and talk quietly or listen." The plants decided to listen. It seems we all liked stories.

"I will tell you one thing, trees provide for people in many ways. All trees grow proudly, and when it is our turn to help, another tree is placed in our honour to keep helping. That is another story." Elm boughed his head to honour all the trees that have helped and all the trees that keep helping.

The very next day, we watched Elm's story come true. Two ladies came in, they picked Spruce up, we knew what was happening as Spruce was in the arms of one lady while the other gave Mr. Green Leaf the paper. Spruce said goodbye, we all said goodbye Spruce, we will miss you and he was gone.

It did not matter what Elm said about not being sad, as we were all sad for ourselves. We would miss him, but that did not mean we weren't happy for him too.

Pine was the saddest of all; he had lost his best friend and he pined about it.

We did try to comfort him, but it didn't help when all Weepy the willow would do was cry. I was sad that I would not be able to listen to the Christmas stories every night. Maybe I could help Pine by asking him about Christmas. I did that just that.

That night and every night after that, Pine and I would talk about Christmas and what a lovey holiday it seemed to be. I wondered if I would ever experience a Christmas as I was not a pine or a spruce or even a fir tree.

One day, a man came in. "Hi, Mr. Green Leaf," he said.

"Oh, hi Bob," Mr. Green Leaf said as he waved.

Bob was looking at Oakley and me when Mr. Green Leaf came over.

"Wow, these trees are beautiful," Bob said.

"Yes, they are. This one's name is Beautiful," Mr. Green Leaf said as he pointed to me, "and this one is special," he said as he pointed to Oakley.

"Psst, I'm special," Oakley whispered.

"Well, I will take them both."

I was so happy. Unlike Spruce and Pine, Oakley and I would get to stay together. We would always be best friends.

Mr. Green Leaf said, "Ok great, you got yourself a beautiful maple tree and a great oak tree. Please take good care of them. You are taking them from their only home they have known the climate in the nursery is much different than being planted outside in the changes of the weather. Make sure you have good soil, plenty of sunshine and water them daily these two get thirsty."

"I know Mr. Green Leaf, I will make sure I only give them the best home and lots of water, but not too much and whatever I need I will come to your nursery where I know you have their interests at heart."

Mr. Green Leaf touched my branch and said, "Bye, Beautiful; I will come see you one day. You too, special oak. I wonder if you will remember me."

I could not answer him as I can only communicate with plants and animals, but if I could have talked to him, I would have said, "I will always remember you; you were so wonderful to me. Goodbye, Mr. Green Leaf."

Oakley, being his typical self, said, "Oh, boo hoo; let's get on with this."

Bob told Mr. Green Leaf he could come see us anytime. They waved goodbye, and as he was taking us out of the nursery, Bob asked, "Did you just water them? They seem a little wet.

"No," Mr. Green Leaf said.

"Oh well, maybe they are crying because they are leaving you."

"Maybe they are, maybe they are sad and scared to leave all they have ever known" Mr. Green Leaf said with a tear in his eye as he waved again.

We were placed in Bobs' truck and then we were off. I wondered where we were going. During our drive, I laughed at Oakley and said, "You cried, ha, ha, you are not so big and tough. I am glad you have a heart. Mr. Green Leaf is a great man, and we were so lucky we had him and each other. It is okay to be sad and to cry."

We pulled up to a lovely house. Bob took us out of the truck and he said, "Welcome to your forever home."

Bob, my new owner, was nice too. He planted us, he watered us, and he called me BEAUTIFUL. I think my name is Beautiful, because Bob calls me that all the time, and so did Mr. Green Leaf. Oakley was like, "What about me, Bob? What about me?"

Bob looked at Oakley and said, "You are an oak tree, and so I am going to call you Oakley." Bob said, "Goodnight Beautiful, goodnight Oakley," and he went into his house.

"Do you believe that?" Oakley said. "Bob called me by my name." He laughed. "Now, that is funny. How did he know my name? You, beautiful? Ha, I am more beautiful than you.""

"Goodnight, Oakley," I said with a sigh.

"Goodnight? Aren't we going to talk as usual?"

"No, it has been a long day and I am tired. I can't wait to see what our forever home is really like," I said.

"Fine. Goodnight Beautiful," Oakley said as he chuckled a bit. "You, beautiful? Ha." We closed our eyes.

The next morning, Bob came out to water us. With him, he had his wife Ginger, his daughter Jill, oh — and a dog named Comehere or it might have been Sit, stay, or No, no, not that. I really think it is Comehere as they call him that a lot.

"These are our new trees," Bob said to his family. "They are beautiful." Ginger said.

Bob laughed and explained, "That is the maple's name and the oak tree is Oakley."

His wife laughed and teased, "You talk to and name your trees?" As she started toward the house, she said, "Let's go." She looked at the dog and said, "Comehere, Jill, let's go. He talks to his trees." She chuckled. "I wonder if they talk back? Crazy old man."

It was wonderful to see outside. Bob told us it was spring. It was different outside when you compared it to the nursery. I could feel the wind blowing slightly through my leaves.

Soon, I began meeting new friends. I already had my leaf friends. I met birds, squirrels, and a caterpillar. They tickled me as they ran up and crawled around on my branches.

One of the birds was a grey jay, his name is Robin.

"Wait, the grey jay is named after another bird?"

"Would you listen Oakley? anyways before I was rudely interrupted the grey jay is the national bird of Canada as of 2016. Oakley jumped in again "Really? I heard our national bird was loonie, ha ha, you know coo coo?" I gave Oakley the look, anyways, I already knew this because the chirpy blue jay Ace told me.

Ace said that he is special bird too. He represents the only Canadian baseball team and is beloved by Canadians everywhere, especially in Toronto, Ontario. Mind you, as much as I loved my new chirpy friend, he chirped really loud and a lot.

It was so different outside. There was what they called weather, and sometimes I got watered by the skies and not by Bob. I could see him standing in his window he would smile at us, but on those days, he could not tell us stories. At least Oakley and my other friends were here. We were their shelter; they were our company. We would tell stories on those nights and pretty much every night. Mack was one of the greatest story tellers, he told us all about trees. He seemed to know everything.

That night, Mack, we call him the informant, said "Oakley, I have a story for you."

"What would you know that I do not? I know everything." He sneered.

Oakley and Mack always fought back and forth about who knew more, little did Oakley know Mack knew one thing Oakley did not.

"Oh yeah?" Mack said, "did you know that one day you will be hosting all those ticklish squirrels? They will love crawling on your branches more than Beautiful', and they will eat all your friends."

"Who is going to eat my friends!? what friends?" Oakley said hysterically.

"Well, if you would listen, I will tell you, you nut!" Mack laughed, nobody else laughed, "oh sorry, you'll know why I laughed when I finish my story. Okay Oakley, you are an Oak Tree."

"Yeah so, what does that have to do with the squirrels?"

"You interrupt too much" one leaf chimed in.

"Well, you are getting new friends NOT anytime soon, but in about 20 years you will grow your first acorn and squirrels love to eat them."

"Really?"

"Yep, so you have a while yet, but it will happen, so enjoy your limited squirrel life now." Mack laughed.

"I will believe it when I see it," Oakley was not impressed.

That night was wonderful everyone told stories, I think we stayed up all night.

It was summer now. This was a hot season, but summer was so much fun with so many more friends. Cardinals, robins, and hummingbirds joined my bird friends, and there were lots of people too. There were a lot of picnics and barbecues. I had grown big enough to provide shade for everyone. They all loved Oakley and me for a spot to get out of the hot sun, and they called me Beautiful.

The kids always wanted to climb us, but Bob said, "Maybe next year they will be stronger and they will be happy to have you play on them." I thought I would love the kids to play with me, but on me? That seemed painful.

Suddenly the picnics and barbecues stopped. It was just Oakley and me. Bob watered us and talked to us every day, and he still called me Beautiful.

The weather was getting cooler. My birds left, my squirrels left, and I was getting lonely.

The caterpillar had already flown away. I know; that freaked me out, too. One minute, Crawly the caterpillar, then one day she snuck up my branches, never to be been seen for two sleeps. I wondered where she had gone. She did not crawl out, that's for sure; she was now a lovely butterfly. She was actually beautiful, but that is my name. When she did leave, she said, "Goodbye, Beautiful and Oakley; thanks for providing me with shelter while I transformed."

"What do you mean transformed?" I asked.

"Silly, you don't recognize me. I am Crawly. I started out a caterpillar. Then, I found a spot to make a cocoon, it was like a warm blanket, and *voilà*! I come out like this! Aren't I beautiful?"

I just nodded my boughs. "Goodbye, Crawly; fly this way sometime."

"I will," she said, and she flew away.

After that, I lost my first leaf. I wondered what was happening. It seemed my leaf friends were changing colours and all leaving me; they were falling to the ground. Oakley was losing his leaf friends too. Bob still called me Beautiful. He explained to us that it was fall. He said that we were stronger than our leaf friends, but they would take care of us by nourishing us for the cold and snowy weather that was coming.

I knew that each time one of my friends started changing colour, it would not be long before we had to say goodbye. As they fell to the ground, wrapping around my trunk, they said, "Goodbye, Beautiful; goodbye, Oakley." It was sad.

We said, "Goodbye."

I only had one leaf friend left. Suddenly, she fell. Before saying goodbye, she said, "You will make new friends soon enough; branches up." I sapped. My sap was so sweet and yummy, I thought that may be why Weepy wept so much.

I had to remain strong, but I still felt lonely. But I still had Oakley, and Bob still talked to us. Bob seemed to know our friends would be back.

It got so cold, and I missed my friends, but thanks to Bob, Oakley, Jill, and even Comehere, I still felt warm and safe. Bob would come out and talk to us and call me Beautiful, but he did not water us. The white stuff on the ground kept us watered. Bob called it snow.

Bob said, "It is winter and it will get cold, but the snow will cover your trunks like a blanket and keep you warm."

We saw a lot of Comehere while the snow was on the ground. I think his name grew longer, because anytime he tried to come near Oakley or myself, Bob would shout, "Nonogetoutofitcomehere!" Wow, what a name.

One day, Bob came out and tied a yellow ribbon around Oakley's trunk. He hung lights on our branches and he told us it was Christmas. This made us think of Spruce and Pine and all the wonderful stories. I wondered if we would get presents too.

The next morning, it was Christmas. Oakley and I looked in Bob's living room window. The whole family was there, and guess who we saw? Just guess, one guess, please? It was Pine from the nursery! He was standing tall and proud, he had lights on him like Oakley and I, and we could hear his thoughts. He was telling us, "It's Christmas Day!" He was so happy. He had so many presents surrounding him, but he still wondered about Spruce. He asked us, "Did he get his Christmas wish too?"

We told him, "Of course he did; he is a Christmas tree, after all." Oh, and we were using telepathy to communicate. That is where you can talk to someone with out talking at all, like mind reading. "Merry Christmas, Pine," Oakley and I said.

Well, it seemed that after Christmas was over, things changed a bit. The snow was watering me, but it seemed to get warmer. During the Winter the snow was watering me it was opposite. Now, I was giving my owner water: sweet water.

Bob gave me a little spout. It did not tickle, but it did not hurt when he put it in. After he got his water from me, he would always say, "Thank you, Beautiful. You are providing me and my family with the most delicious maple syrup."

I was so happy that I was making him as happy as he made me.

"Oakley, how come I got a spout, and you didn't?" I asked.

"It seems you have sweet sap that makes maple syrup and I don't. All trees have sap, but yours is the best. I should know; I sneak some when you sleep," he said as he tickled me with his branches.

"No need to sneak it; we are friends. Help yourself." I said.

"Thanks, buddy." Oakley almost teared up but then he looked away. It took a long time, but spring had finally arrived.

Bob kept telling us stories that always started with, "Hi, Beautiful; hi, Oakley." We were so lucky to have such a smart and wonderful owner.

If I could have talked to him, I would have said, "Thank you for keeping us company through the cold winter. You made us feel warm and safe."

Suddenly, something happened: my friends started coming back.

My leaf friends were growing. They were relatives of my friends from last year; one of the leaves told me so. I knew who he was because of where he was on my branch. He was the informant, just like his daddy Mack.

I would figure out who was who soon enough, but for now, I was just so happy to see my friends.

My old friends were back, including the squirrels who tickled my branches and the birds — even the chirpy blue jays. Friends old and new not only made me happy, but it made Bob and Oakley happy too.

Oakley was not a fan of the ticklish squirrels, but you could tell he was happy to see our friends.

Bob began watering us and talking to us as always. He called me Beautiful, and I gave him my sweet water. He was always so grateful.

He whispered to my trunk, "I told you they would be back and Mr. Green Leaf called and he is going to come for a visit, just then Mr. Green Leaf showed up.

"Hi Bob," Mr. Green Leaf waved.

"Hi Mr. Green Leaf," Bob waved back.

"Wow you have done a wonderful job with the trees! Look at them, they are so big and strong. They must be producing a lot of fresh air for all of us."

"Yes, they are Mr. Green Leaf and Beautiful is giving us wonderful maple syrup, would you like to try some?"

"Yes please"

They both came over and tasted my sap, Mr. Green Leaf for the first time, Bob just because he loved it.

"Delicious Beautiful, I knew you would grow to be the perfect tree."

Bob and Mr. Green Leaf spent the afternoon talking to us and to each other about trees. When Mr. Green Leaf left he said goodbye to Oakley and I and in our quiet way we said, "Bye Mr. Green Leaf, it was wonderful to see you."

Hearing the birds chirping, seeing the people playing and the visit with Mr. Green Leaf brought great happiness. Everything was back.

Bob started to feed the birds and the squirrels peanuts; he even put out a bird bath for the birds. They loved it. The birds would drink from their bird bath and swim in it on hot days. Bob also hung a bird house on one of my branches and he said to the squirrels, "Stay out of it!" He smiled when he said it.

We were all so lucky to have each other. Bob was always there for us, and we made him happy too. He kept us safe, happy, warm, and loved so that my friends would return.

It is playtime again and I am going to love every minute of it. I know it will end again, but it will all return come spring. I think SPRING is my favourite time of year. I feel loved, helpful, and very respected.

I AM ONE LUCKY MAPLE TREE.

It is time to play now. BYE, my new friends.

CPSIA information can be obtained
at www.ICGtesting.com
Printed in the USA
BVHW022051121221
623840BV00001B/1

9 780228 846475